HARD SENSE
IN SOFT
WORDS

Hard Sense in Soft Words

Sayings from the Great Oral Tradition of Ireland

G. B. Ryan

M. Evans and Company, Inc.
New York

M. Evans and Company, Inc.
216 East 49th Street
New York, New York 10017

ISBN 0-87131-992-6

Book design and typesetting by Rik Lain Schell

Printed in the United States of America

CONTENTS

Foreword

Before the arrival in Ireland of Christian monks in the fifth century, sagas, poems, sayings and genealogies were stored in human memory. People with the ability to memorize large parts of this cultural store had a special status in society. In today's terminology, these individuals were protected as living memory banks or data storage centers. They knew all the glories of your clan, and could detail the misdeeds and failings of your enemies. They also had an immediate practical use. As poets and storytellers traveled from place to place unharmed, they brought news with them of what was happening in the lands surrounding yours. They heard rumors of who was preparing a cattle raid or who was getting ready to avenge an insult. They had banqueted with local kings and chiefs. They could assess their current fierceness, power and wealth, the beauty of their women, the loyalty and number of warriors present, and the quality and quantity of their arms and horses.

After leaving your banqueting hall to continue their wandering, they could make widely known your heroics, high style, and generosity, spreading envy among your friends and fear among your enemies. But if they had suffered some lack of hospitality or respect as your guests, they could also make fun of you. Uncomplimentary remarks, neatly packaged for easy memory, spread only mockery and disdain.

Things didn't change greatly after the monks built libraries and scriptoria in their monasteries. They mostly copied sacred texts in Latin and left pagan Gaelic works to be memorized in the traditional ways. The monks did not put Gaelic stories into writing until the tenth century at the earliest. By the time they were recorded, most of the pre-Christian sagas and poems had survived six hundred years of Christianity. While some stories show obvious signs of alteration to fit later beliefs, a large number survived in what seem to be their original Celtic attitudes. How old these stories are is anyone's guess. Some may go back to the Iron

Age, while others may have originated in the
Christian era. Like the ancient Hebrews, ancient
Celtic rulers kept track of the names of their male
ancestors over an incredible number of generations. The son of . . . the son of . . . the son of . . .
The Celts had no other dating system. Patrick
returned to Ireland in 432 A.D. Before that date,
only genealogies give an idea of when people
lived. It's often impossible to say whether an
event took place two hundred or seven hundred
years before Patrick. The ancient Celts' fondness
for exaggeration doesn't help.

The Romans conquered the Celts across Europe,
but Ireland was never part of the Roman Empire.
This accounts for the survival of Celtic culture long
after it had been Romanized elsewhere. Patrick
himself is believed to have been a Romanized Celt.
After the arrival of Christianity and Roman influ-
ence, Latin and Gaelic coexisted for centuries in
Ireland. But in Ireland, the Gaelic language and
Celtic traditions remained dominant.

Daniel Corkery claimed that Ireland differs from
most European countries because it was not directly affected by Europe's three great formative influ-

ences: the Roman Empire, the Renaissance, and the Industrial Revolution. While perhaps oversimplified and extreme, this is a useful perspective.

The Celtic way of life survived in the Irish countryside into the late nineteenth century. In the absence of the industrialization that caused so many social and economic changes elsewhere, people continued to rely on the wisdom of traditional ways. For another hundred years, into the early 1990s, many Irish people living on the land and in villages or small towns dwelt relatively free of urban influences. These people will be familiar with most or all of the sayings in this book.

Not everyone you meet in the Irish countryside today has kept in touch with the Celtic tradition. On the other hand, don't assume that someone with a mechanized farm who watches soccer on television has lost touch with the old ways. Keep in mind that Celtic warriors, had they the choice, would have driven Ferraris, and Grace O'Malley, the pirate queen, would have worn Prada.

Triads are an early Irish form of proverb. Each triad names a characteristic that three things have in common. In the estimation of their translator, Kuno Meyer, these triads were collected toward the end of the ninth century:

- **Three slender things that best support the world: the slender stream of milk from the cow's dug into the pail, the slender blade of green corn upon the ground, the slender thread over the hand of a skilled woman.**
- **Three fewnesses that are better than plenty: a fewness of fine words, a fewness of cows in grass, a fewness of friends around good ale.**
- **Three nurses of theft: a wood, a cloak, night.**
- **Three false sisters: perhaps, maybe, I daresay.**
- **Three timid brothers: hush, stop, listen.**
- **Three keys that unlock thoughts: drunkenness, trustfulness, love.**

The only triad in this book, apart from those quoted above, is number 61. In print, the triad format quickly becomes tedious. But computer users will recognize the triad as a convenient and effective way of organizing data for retrieval from memory. A thousand years ago, men who had memorized hundreds of triads may have wandered from kingdom to kingdom, answering questions or giving advice by quoting from memory. Over the centuries, this folk wisdom—sayings in memorable form—presumably evolved into the sayings in this book and others like them.

Do all the proverbs here originate in Ireland? It's impossible to say. Probably not. But very nearly all the sayings in this book have been translated from Gaelic (not by me), and so they can be said to be part of Irish oral culture.

What can be said to be distinctive about the Celtic outlook? Abbey Theatre playwright Sean O'Casey gave us insight in his remark that a tragic play provides an incomplete view of life. He believed that tragicomedy provides a far more encompassing look at the way we really live. The Celtic outlook can be said to be tragicomic. It goes without saying, of course, that a lot of Irish people see nothing to smile at in their lives. All the same, a remarkable number have a highly developed sense of the ridiculous in other people's lives—and often enough in their own.

By *Celtic* and *Irish*, I refer to culture rather than race. We have only to glance at history to understand that every Irish person's genome is highly seasoned with Norse, Norman, and Saxon genes.

Irish sayings are rarely inspired by simple optimism. Blue skies in Ireland normally contain a percentage of cloud cover, and people acknowledge this fact. Their experience suggests that when something sounds too good to be true, it usually is. They recognize that we are rarely driven by a single heroic or demonic impulse. Where they see strength, they know there is weakness, too. Where there is altruism, they expect some selfishness also. The Irish tend not to trust shiny packaging and high-sounding claims.

Collections of Irish proverbs in the English language often make use of Victorian headings, such as "Fortitude" or "Solitude" or "Trustworthiness." This kind of organization works for straightforward and idealistic sayings. The problem with Irish sayings is that many have a sting in the tail. They can't be relied upon to be tame and polite—

and sit quietly in a Victorian category. I've tried arranging this selection in a different way. A story or incident goes with each group of sayings. Sometimes the introductory story or incident is only very loosely connected with the sayings that follow. The story's function is to act as background rather than to emphasize some moral or ethical point. The sources of many of these stories and incidents can be found in Background Reading.

Reknowned collections of proverbs were made by the Rev. Ulick Bourke, Henry Morris, Micheal O Longain, and T. F. O'Rahilly. In the Gaelic language, Munster proverbs were collected by T. O'Donoghue, Ulster proverbs by E. Ua Muirgheasa, and Connacht proverbs by T. S. O Maille. I am indebted to the work of the present-day scholars Laurence Flanagan, Sean Gaffney, and Seamus Cashman.

Will this book help you lose weight? Yes, if you walk very quickly while reading it.

The monk and his pet cat

While most of the manuscripts penned by Irish monks before 1100 are in Latin, the comments in the margins are usually in Gaelic. These comments sometimes consist of a short original poem by the monk copying the Latin text, a task that would strike most of us as boring and laborious. But one monk likened his work to that of his pet cat. This Gaelic poem is in a ninth-century Irish manuscript now in a monastery in Carinthia, Austria. The poem begins:

> My cat Pangur Bawn and I
> Have each our special work.
> His mind is set on hunting mice.
> Stalking words, I sit for hours.

The simplicity of this poem, written more than a thousand years ago, brings to mind the pleasure

of petting a cat while watching television in a
rodent-free room. But this cat and monk are at
work. In rural Ireland to this day, cats still have
their work and an essential place in the farmyard.
Yet beyond all the purposefulness, the monk's
affection for the cat is clear.

Neither reward nor domesticity affects the free
spirit of a cat. Perhaps the monk, who has entered
voluntary bondage to save his soul, unwillingly
admires that.

1. A cat is her own best adviser.
2. A cat is bold in a place where she is well
   known.
3. What would you expect from a cat but a
   kitten?
4. What would the son of a cat do but catch a
   mouse?
5. Cats like fish but don't like to wet their
   paws.

Finn's Hounds

Finn Mac Cool and Conan relaxed on the Hill of Allen. Below them, they watched Finn's two huge staghounds hunt. The hounds were famous for their cunning and intelligence. It was said that they could read Finn's mind without him uttering a word.

"Someone told me those hounds are your cousins," Conan said.

"They are," Finn acknowledged.

Some of the great druids were shape-changers, transforming at will into various animals. Warriors like Finn and Conan were wary of any bird or animal they saw behaving strangely, knowing that it could be a druid spying on them for an enemy. Worse still, it could be the work of the Sidhe, the fairy people who lived under the ancient forts and who were capable of very strange things. Conan suspected that something like this was involved.

"How are these hounds related to you?" he asked, hoping not to offend the ferocious Finn but curious all the same.

Finn told him how his mother brought her sister Tuiren to visit him at the Hill of Allen. Tuiren wanted to marry an Ulster chief and asked Finn to send word to her future husband to be nice to her. Finn knew that the Ulster chief already had a woman of the Sidhe as his lover. He sent along a few members of the Fianna—the warrior band that roamed Ireland dispensing justice as they saw fit—to accompany Tuiren to her wedding. The Ulster chief, knowing that Tuiren was Finn's aunt and that Finn was leader of the Fianna, approached them and politely inquired if Finn had sent good wishes. The men from the Fianna said all Finn wanted was that his aunt come to see him from time to time. No problem, the Ulster chief assured them.

In the succeeding months, the woman of the Sidhe restrained her jealousy—until Tuiren became pregnant. That was more than she could bear. She lured Tuiren away and changed her into a staghound. Then she brought the staghound to a

chief who lived in distant Galway and who was
known to hate all kinds of dogs.

"Why are you giving me this staghound?" he
asked. "I hate dogs."

"Finn asked me to bring it to you," the woman
of the Sidhe said.

The Galway chief saw he was being made an
offer he couldn't refuse. "If Finn wants me to
have this dog," he said, "I'll take it out of respect
for Finn."

While she was with the Galway chief, Tuiren
gave birth to two pups, which, Finn said, were the
staghounds they were now watching as they
hunted.

Conan glanced at Finn. "That would make these
hounds your first cousins," he said.

"Yes," Finn said happily. "Bran and Sceolan are
their names."

"That's good to know," Conan said. "How did
they join you here?"

Finn said that when Tuiren vanished without a
trace, the Ulster chief tried to keep it quiet, hoping
she would show up again before Finn heard about
it. But word leaked out. Finn sent a Fianna man,

with instructions to bring back either Tuiren or
the Ulster chief's head. The Ulster chief begged the
Fianna man for time, saying that if he couldn't
bring her to Finn alive and well, he'd show up
himself to offer Finn his head. The Fianna man
had a soft heart and gave the chief a break.

By now, the Ulster chief had guessed his girl-
friend from the Sidhe was involved. Explaining
that his life depended on it, he pleaded with her to
bring Tuiren to Finn. She went to Galway, brought
Tuiren to Finn and changed her back into human
shape. Tuiren told Finn she had given birth to pups
in Galway. So Finn sent the woman of the Sidhe
to fetch them. When Finn saw the two marvelous
young staghounds, he forbade the woman of the
Sidhe from changing them into human shape, saying he liked them just as they were.

The Hill of Allen is about four miles northwest
of Newbridge, County Kildare. People walking the
lonely bog roads there, very late at night or in the
early morning hours, often hear deep growls and
the sounds of two large creatures running. Most
of these people stay very quiet, until the sounds
have faded away into the dark.

6. Kick my dog and you kick me.

7. It's hard to teach an old dog to dance.

8. Keep the bone and the dog will follow you.

9. Hit a dog with a bone and he won't growl.

10. Draw your hand out of a dog's mouth as gently as you can.

11. Lie with dogs and you rise with fleas.

12. A hound finds his food with his feet.

13. Every hound is a pup till he hunts.

14. The hound is not found until the deer is gone.

15. Better the leavings of a dog than the leavings of a mocker.

16. The hungry hound thinks not of its whelps.

17. The dogs haven't eaten up the end of the year yet.

A horse called Papillon

O n April 9, 2000, a day after he had won the Grand National at Aintree, England, the world's greatest steeple-chase, Papillon was back home in Kill, County Kildare. The horse was accompanied by his trainer on his victory circuit of the village, led by a bag-piper playing "A Nation Once Again" and other patriotic tunes. Admirers reached out to rub the nose that had been first past the winning post.

"Just watch his ould hind legs," the trainer warned them, as reported in the *Irish Times*. "He's a quiet ould Christian, but with all the excite-ment, you never know."

In his un-Christian moments, according to the trainer, the horse was known to be a "leery ould bugger." But on this day, Papillon never raised a hoof in anger.

"Isn't he gorgeous," one woman said.

On a stage built in front of the Dew Drop Inn,

the trainer thanked the horse's woman owner, remarking that he had shared many a drink with her after hours in the pub behind them. He also thanked his right-hand man at the stables. The right-hand man, who was celebrating a big winning bet on the race, clambered up on Papillon's back.

"He was never a stylish jockey," the trainer told the *Irish Times* reporter. "But with a few drinks in him, he's a brave one."

At this point, the owner announced from the stage that the horse was standing everyone a drink, in either of the village pubs. The newspaper noted that this was a risky offer in an Irish village, even a small one. But after collecting 290,000 pounds prize money, the owner seemed confident she could handle the bill.

18. A nod is as good as a wink to a blind horse.

19. Put a beggar on horseback and he'll go at a gallop.

20. Everyone lays a burden on the willing horse.
21. A tattered foal can grow into a splendid horse.
22. The best jockeys are in the stands.

Nancy, Lily, and Josephine

The intelligence war that Michael Collins waged on British forces in Ireland during the Troubles did much to dissuade the London government from continuing to seek a military solution in Ireland. British officers in Dublin came to realize that they were playing a deadly game with someone they did not know and could not see—but someone who was watching them. The British hunted and laid traps for Collins everywhere. At one time in 1919, they conducted more than a thousand house searches per week, with attendant intimidation and damage. They never found him or the sources of his information. It never occurred to them to question three industrious ladies named Nancy, Lily, and Josephine.

When Collins heard that his cousin Nancy O'Brien had been put in charge of handling coded intelligence messages at British headquarters in

Dublin, he could hardly believe it. He was genuinely shocked that a close relative of the most wanted man in Ireland—himself—could be appointed to this position. "In the name of Jaysus," he said, "how did these people ever get an empire?" As Collins increasingly exposed her to danger and overworked her, Nancy proved to be daring and resourceful. She copied important messages by hand and carried them out in her underclothes. She searched intelligence files for requested information, including files located in areas where she had no right to be. Her suburban apartment was used in the night hours as a dropoff point by spies and informers. After going from Dublin to Cork by train for her father's funeral, Nancy was assisted from her carriage by a British officer, who joked in a gentlemanly way about the weight of her bags. Collins had persuaded her to fill them with guns and ammunition for Cork rebels.

Lily Merin was a typist at Dublin Castle. She prepared reports on security and counter-insurgency, which reached Collins almost as soon as her superiors. When the authorities realized

that they were losing the intelligence war, they
brought their top undercover agents to Dublin.
Their mission was to penetrate the IRA intelligence operation. While Lily didn't know their
names, she knew the faces of men who frequently
showed up at Dublin Castle to see British spy-
masters. During her lunch hour, she walked in
fashionable streets on the arm of a Collins man,
giving his arm a special squeeze any time she saw
a British agent approach. Once they were recognized, Collins fed disinformation to these agents
and otherwise played with them before he
pounced. Many learned the cost of the glance
they had exchanged with a pretty woman.

Josephine Marchmont was chief clerk at British
military headquarters in Cork. Her father had
been in the Royal Irish Constabulary, and her
Welsh husband had recently given his life for
Britain in the Great War. No one could question
her loyalty to the Crown. One day a canteen
worker found her in tears over an untouched
meal and heard how her mother-in-law in Wales
refused to return her two young sons. A few days
later, a handsome stranger approached her on the

street, identified himself as an IRA man and offered, in exchange for future information, to kidnap her two sons and bring them to live in a farmhouse outside Cork city, where she could visit and stay with them as often and as long as she liked. Her conflicts and turmoil must have been great, but as they say in Cork, nothing is as strong as a mother's love. The handsome IRA man made good on his promise, and she made good on hers. After the Troubles, they married.

23. **Eight views, eight versions.**
24. **There are two ways of telling every story, and twelve ways of singing a song.**
25. **A sweet voice does not cause tooth decay.**
26. **A blind person is no judge of color.**

The Children of Lir

The Tuatha De Danaan (People of Dana) ruled Ireland before the coming of the Celts. After the Celts invaded, they went to live underground and became known as the Sidhe (fairies). These events took place while they still ruled Ireland. One of their kings had a daughter married to Lir. Their oldest child was a girl, and they had three sons, including twins. All were still very young when their mother died. Lir would have killed himself out of grief but for the sake of the children.

After his daughter's death, the king gave Lir his foster daughter, Aoife, as a wife and mother to the children. Aoife was very beautiful. But she felt she had to compete with the children for the affections of Lir and their grandfather, her foster father. Her love of the children turned to hatred. One morning when she was taking them to visit their grandfather, the king, she ordered her chariot stopped. She took her accompanying warriors to one side and ordered them to kill the children. They refused. Apart from liking the children, they feared their father and grandfather. In a fury, Aoife got back in the chariot and they went on.

"What's happening?" Lir's daughter asked.

"Nothing," Aoife snapped.

Her younger brothers were oblivious, but the oldest child sensed that something was wrong.

Aoife ordered the chariot stopped again while they were traveling along the shore of Lough Derravaragh, near present-day Castlepollard in County Westmeath. She suggested the children might like a swim in the lake. The three boys immediately ran and jumped into the water, but the girl hung back, watchful. Aoife ordered her into the water. She went reluctantly.

While they were in the water, Aoife cast a spell on them that ended with her shouting: "Waterfowl will be your only family from now on, and may your crying mingle with the cries of flocks of birds!"

They became four swans on the lake.

"Why did you do this to us?" one swan called in

the voice of Lir's daughter. "Give us back our
shapes."

The other three swans wailed and pleaded with
Aoife in the boys' voices.

"My father will find out you did this and punish
you!" the swan who was Lir's daughter threatened.

Aoife said nothing and turned her back on
them. She realized that what the girl said was
true. Lir would be furious. So would the king.
Besides, listening to their pleading, she felt a little
sorry for them. Had she the power, she might
even have reversed the spell. But this spell was
too powerful for her to reverse.

"Please tell us when we can have our shapes
back, Aoife," Lir's daughter pleaded. "Don't make
us be swans forever."

Turning to them once more, Aoife said, "You'll
be swans for nine hundred summers and winters
and can never step ashore. You'll spend the first
three hundred summers and winters here on
Lough Derravaragh, the next three hundred on
the Sea of Moyle, and the last three hundred on
Inish Glora in the western ocean. When a western
king marries a southern queen and you hear a

bell pealing, the spell will be lifted."

Aoife strode to her chariot and rode away. The four swans paddled around, crying with children's voices.

When Aoife arrived at the royal fort, the king welcomed his foster daughter and asked, "Where are the children? I thought you were bringing them to see me."

"I wanted to," she said, "but Lir is jealous of their love for you and kept them at home."

The king flew into a rage and swore that words would never pass between Lir and him again. As he grew more calm, he wondered what had really caused Lir's behavior. Without Aoife's knowledge, he sent a messenger to summon Lir and his children.

On hearing that Aoife was at the king's without his children, Lir had a premonition that something was terribly wrong. He set out without delay. The children, seeing their father and his warriors ride along the lake shore, flew and landed on the water near them. They called to their father. Lir stopped his horse and listened. The children called to him again. He heard the voices of his children. So did his men. But there was no one there—only four swans on the water.

Lir dismounted and walked to the water's edge. The swans paddled toward him. They told him who they were and said they could not come on land. Lir waded out and embraced each of them. As he stroked her head and feathers, his daughter tearfully told him what had happened.

As Lir, standing chest deep in water, heard that no power could undo the spell making them swans for nine hundred summers and winters, his head bowed and his shoulders sagged. The warriors stood at the lake edge, tears running down their scarred faces.

Seeing how distraught they had made their father and his warriors, the children sang. Their enchanted songs comforted the men. They camped along the shore that night, and the children sang them to sleep.

Next morning, Lir said goodbye to his children at the lake edge. Then he rode on to meet the king. Lir accused Aoife, while the king listened. When she could not deny what she had done, the king flew into a rage and shouted at her, "I will cast a spell on you, making you a demon of the air, doomed to be driven forever with clouds though the sky."

The king cast the spell on her. A powerful wind lifted Aoife off the ground and carried her high into the air like a leaf. She was lifted higher and higher, all the time screaming above the sounds of the wind. They watched her become a tiny speck and finally disappear from view. In this part of Westmeath, on stormy nights, she can still sometimes be heard shrieking above high winds.

For three hundred summers and winters, Lir and the king and both their courts visited and talked with the children on Lough Derravaragh. One day, Lir's daughter broke the news that it was time for them to leave for the Sea of Moyle. This was far away, where they had no friends. Knowing they would probably never see the children again, Lir and the king were heartbroken.

"Let's sing them to sleep," the girl said to her brothers. "Then, while they're asleep, we'll quietly fly away."

This they did.

The Sea of Moyle, between Ireland and Scotland, was cold and lonely. Only seals heard their songs in this place. Once, in a gale, they became separated and each thought the others dead. One winter night, the sea froze and they were caught in the ice. They could not free themselves and nearly died of hunger and cold, before being rescued by a thaw.

Friends of Lir and the king passed by one day and recognized the swans by their talk. They told the children that their father and grandfather were well, apart from missing them very much.

Hearing about home overcame the girl swan's emotions. She broke into long lamentations about the love, pleasure, and comfort of home, all of which were denied them on this desolate shore. Feeling sorry for her, the people promised to bring Lir news of his children.

The girl swan pulled herself together. "Tell him we are well," she said.

At long last, the three hundred summers and winters were up in this terrible place. They prepared to fly to Inish Glora, on the western ocean.

"If we fly south before flying west," Lir's daughter said to her brothers, "we could pass by our father's fort and see him."

They agreed that this was a great idea. The four birds flew southward until they recognized the land beneath them. But then they became confused. Some things were familiar, yet other things seemed changed. And they couldn't find their father's fort. They circled round and round without being able to locate it. Finally they landed on a pond that looked exactly like the one near their father's home. But only broken earthworks and piles of stones lay near this pond. Weeds grew everywhere.

The truth dawned upon them all at once. They looked around them and remembered all the things they had seen here—kings and queens feasting, warriors exulting, poets chanting, and priests calling upon powerful gods. They could hear laughter, harp music, and hounds hunting where now only the wind blew through nettles. On the pond next to these silent ruins, they sang together of their loves and sorrows. Then they rose from the water, circled the ruins once and flew to the west.

Inish Glora was a small rocky island in a sheltered bay off the ocean. At the center of the island
was a small freshwater lake, which became their
home. Here they sheltered from great ocean
storms. Although the seas were more powerful
here, the seasons were warmer than on the Sea of
Moyle. The children flew up and down the coast,
exploring other bays and islands. They talked a lot
to one another and continued to sing, particularly
when they were on their lake on Inish Glora.
Birds crowded onto the few trees and bushes to
hear their songs. Although the children did not
know it, they were heard by humans, too. Word
spread along this sparsely inhabited coast of the
presence of four talking swans. A few remembered what had happened to the children of Lir.
So many summers and winters passed, the
children found it hard to keep count.

One summer evening, they flew back to the
lake after having been farther south for some
weeks. They landed on the lake water as the sun
set beyond the ocean. They tucked their heads
under theirs wings and slept, floating gently on
the calm water.

At first light, a loud noise rang out across the lake and woke the children. They were so frightened, they almost took to the air. It sounded to them like giants fighting with mighty iron weapons. Yet they could see that this sound was coming from a small stone building near the lake that had not been there a few weeks previously when they left. Next to it, a bald man dressed in coarse cloth was hitting a metal tongue inside an inverted metal bowl. Seeing that this man had no weapons and appeared to be of low social rank, the children paddled toward him. A little haughtily, Lir's daughter asked him what he thought he was doing.

"From your voice," he said, "I can tell that you are Fionnuala."

He knew all their names and what Aoife had done to them. He told them about the coming of the Celts and how the Tuatha De Danaan had gone underground. Lir and the king were long since dead, he said. He himself was a holy man, a hermit, who had renounced the world.

"Why did you make that loud sound?" Fionnuala asked.

"That's my bell," the hermit said. "I ring it to thank God."

"Which god?" one of the brothers asked.

"I have only one," the hermit said.

"We have lots," the brother boasted, ruffling his feathers.

"Much good they have done you," the hermit said.

The brother floated away, annoyed. Were it not for his sister's presence, he might have used his wings to knock down this old fool and used his beak to slash his bald head. But she was upset enough after hearing of their father's death. He didn't want to upset her more. Besides, he desired to hear more of what this hermit had to say. Floating back into earshot, he tried not to let his interest show.

"Has a king married a queen recently?" Fionnuala asked the hermit.

"The western king is soon to marry the southern queen," he said. "Why?'

"Because we have heard a bell peal," she answered mysteriously.

The hermit guessed that the spell upon the

children of Lir was about to be lifted. He decided
he would be the one to baptize them as
Christians. But could he baptize talking swans?
People would say he had gone mad out here
alone on this western isle. He would have to wait
until the swans transformed back into people. In
the meantime, so they could not leave, he linked
the swans together with a silver chain and
attached one end of it to the lake shore.

But word spread of the hermit's plans. When
the southern queen arrived to marry the western
king, she heard about the four talking swans and
asked for them as a gift. When the western king
said he wanted no dealings with magic creatures
or solitary monks, the southern queen threatened
to go home if he didn't grant her request. The
king sent warriors to collect the swans. But the
hermit refused to hand them over. The warriors
were afraid to seize entranced creatures against
the will of a holy man. They returned to the king.
He scorned their lack of courage and said he
would do it himself.

When the king came to Inish Glora, he swept
aside the protesting hermit with one hand. "She

won't marry me till I give her these talking swans," he said.

He walked to the lake edge and picked up the silver chain. Then, one by one, he dragged the four swans, wings flapping, onto land.

The swans were on the grass for less than a minute when their white feathers began to drop off. The falling feathers revealed the wrinkled skin of a very old woman and three very old men, chained together, lying naked on the grass.

The king fled in horror to his boat.

Seeing that they were dying, the hermit baptized them with water from the lake and comforted them as best he could. After they had died, he buried them together, with Fionnuala's arms outstretched like protecting wings over the bodies of her brothers.

27. When the sky falls, we'll all catch larks.
28. An old bird is not caught with chaff.
29. It's hard to drive a bird out of a bush if he's not in it.

30. When the old cock crows, the young one learns.
31. A black hen lays white eggs.
32. Eating and complaining like a greedy hen.
33. She never sells her hens on a wet day.
34. A wild goose never laid a tame egg.
35. Don't leave the fox minding the geese.
36. All business like the woman with one duck.
37. A bird flies away from every brood.
38. Every bird as he has been reared, said the cuckoo.
39. Every bird is melodious in his own tree.

Bend with the tree that bends with you

Tristan, a young nobleman sent to Ireland to fetch the beautiful princess Isolde for marriage to a Welsh prince, fell in love with her, and she with him. On arrival in Wales, they fled together and lived in the woods. The Welsh prince tracked them down. Tristan walked among the prince's armed men without drawing his sword, and not a man would strike him down for loving the beautiful Isolde.

Finally Tristan stood in front of the Welsh prince. The prince knew that he would have to face Tristan in single combat now or let him go. He said he was sure that he would win, but in doing so, he might suffer wounds that would interfere with his future physical enjoyment of Isolde. Instead, he said, he would seek justice from the king.

The king called both men before him and heard
their stories. In judgment, he gave Isolde to one
man while there were leaves on the trees, and to
the other while there were none. Because night
was longest and there was more time for love-
making when there were *no* leaves on the trees,
the prince chose that. To his surprise, Tristan read-
ily agreed.

Since it was still summer then, Tristan returned
to Isolde. In November, the prince's men came to
fetch her. They pointed to the bare branches over
their heads and dead leaves under their feet.
Tristan shook his head and took them to see holly,
pines and yews. He told them to come back when
those branches were bare.

Isolde laughed and promised Tristan her love for
him would be as evergreen as those trees.

40. A soft twig outlasts a stubborn tree.
**41. When the twig hardens, it's difficult to
    bend.**

42. The tree blown around the most may not be the first to fall.
43. Don't go between the tree and its bark.
44. A beautiful tree can bear bitter fruit.
45. There's no forest without enough under-growth to burn it.
46. It takes an oak wedge to split an oak.
47. The tree remains, but not the hand that planted it.

Every ocean has another tide

On a rocky headland on the Atlantic coast, the windows of the houses face away from the ocean. There's more protection from gale-force winds that way. Another reason is that most of these families have had fishermen lost at sea, and to them the Atlantic is not a pretty sight. You can tell Dubliners' weekend escapes and tourist cottages by their big picture windows looking out on the ocean. The view is much the same from all of them—small, stone-walled fields containing a few sheep, waves breaking on the rocky shore, and then a vast expanse of ocean. People here like to say that the next parish westward is Boston.

In a field in front of one house, hulks of abandoned cars spoil the view. The wrecked cars seem to be spaced deliberately in the field to occupy as much of the view as possible. The house was built by a wealthy Dublin businessman, who comes with his family for weekends. The field in front of the house is owned by a local farmer. This farmer feels that the Dublin businessman insulted him. He has asked for an apology. The Dubliner stands by what he said and claims he owes no apology.

At some point the car wrecks appeared in the field. The farmer says they will stay there until he gets an apology or until they rust away. The Dubliner has been seen using binoculars to study the rate of car metal corrosion by sea salt. He says he can wait.

48. **Ships are often lost near harbor.**
49. **There are still fish in the sea better than any that have been caught.**
50. **Pity the man who drowned in the storm, for after the rain comes sunshine.**
51. **The sea does not wait for a man with a load.**
52. **A spring tide does not wait for women's conversation.**
53. **Shallow water makes the biggest splash.**

Are you a witch?
Are you a fairy?

his wife, whose body had been possessed by a fairy, rose from her bed and walked out the door around midnight. That was on Friday, March 15, 1895. He had been asleep at the time, her husband said. His name was Michael Cleary. A barrel maker, he lived in a small house on a country road near the village of Drangan in County Tipperary. His wife's name was Bridget. Since her disappearance, he had been going every night to a nearby fairy ring, where he expected to see her pass by on a white horse. He knew he had the courage to fight off the fairies and rescue her.

"Gone with the fairies" was a traditional belief used to explain things ranging from unexplained absences to being emotionally disturbed. Most people used the phrase in a sarcastic or humorous way. The local police showed almost no belief in the possibility. They had heard stories that

Bridget, who was twenty-five or twenty-six, outgoing, and very good looking, was having an affair with an egg trader. When she didn't return, reasoning that her husband might have killed her, they searched for her body.

On March 22, they found it in a shallow grave not far from her home. She had been burned to death. Her husband and eight others were charged.

Michael Cleary maintained that the body found was not that of his wife, but a fairy changeling or imposter. He had known this woman was not his wife because she was two inches taller and had a more polite manner. Family members, neighbors and even a local priest had been involved in a nine-day "fairy trial," during which Cleary repeatedly questioned the unfortunate woman as to whether she was a fairy or his wife. He tried to expel the alleged fairy with spells, herbal potions, prayers, and finally fire. Cleary admitted to killing the fairy. But he claimed that his wife was still alive and he could get her back, if only they would release him from jail.

Newspapers carried lurid accounts of the "witch burning." This worked well with the British notion that Irish natives were too primitive to govern themselves and that it was too early to grant Home Rule. Accordingly, the prosecutor ignored evidence of the dead woman's affair and played up the supernatural aspects of the case. This allowed Cleary, when found guilty, to escape hanging. To this day, no one can say for sure whether he really believed his wife had been taken by the fairies or was covering up a vengeful killing. He was released after fifteen years and emigrated to Canada.

Bridget's memorial is a children's song. Its simplicity masks a terrible event.

> Are you a witch?
> Are you a fairy?
> Are you the wife
> Of Michael Cleary?

54. Self-love is blind.
55. A whistling woman and a crowing hen would raise the devil out of his den.

56. Even if she put her hair under his feet, it wouldn't satisfy him.

57. The man that stays out late, his dinner cools.

58. It takes a foolish woman to know a foolish man.

59. A man is in trouble who doesn't have the advice of a caring wife.

60. Marry a woman from the glen and you marry the whole glen.

61. There are three kinds of men who don't understand women: young men, old men, and middle-aged men.

May I see
you gray and
combing your
children's hair

arsh's Library, near St. Patrick's Cathedral in Dublin, is a high-ceilinged place with ornately carved dark wood shelves. Visitors there sometimes pass an arthritic old clergyman rooting around among the thousands of large, ancient, hand-bound books. Most visitors make no comment about the old man searching among the books. Those who do may not be told they have just seen Archbishop Narcissus Marsh, who founded the library in 1707.

What brings His Grace back so frequently? So far, no one seems to have asked him directly. From his actions, he appears to be searching for something rather than simply browsing through the books. Many believe he is looking for a letter from a niece he raised. She wanted to marry a sea captain. The archbishop said no and did all he could to prevent the couple from seeing each other. They eloped. As the girl left for a new life in foreign lands, she told a servant she had left a letter for her uncle, explaining everything and begging his forgiveness, in a book in his library. Archbishop Marsh never searched for it in his lifetime.

On your visit, should a letter slip from a volume you take down from a shelf, please hand it unread to the elderly clergyman riffling through pages nearby.

62. An angel in the street, a devil in the home.
63. As fingers come in different lengths, children have their own ways of thinking.
64. Give the dainty bit to the sickly child.
65. April showers strengthen the buttercups.
66. The thing the child sees is what the child does.

67. A hereditary disposition is stronger than an education.
68. He got it from nature, as a pig gets rooting in the ground.

There's no
fireside like your
own fireside

A no-nonsense military man who had spent his life guarding Queen Victoria's far-flung colonies, Col. Bushe retired in the middle of the nineteenth century. He came to live at Glencairn, a mansion on the river Blackwater, in County Waterford, near Lismore. A bachelor, he lived alone in the big house. He didn't want to be alone, but the local people he hired as servants to take care of the mansion refused to sleep there anymore after the first few weeks. Instead, they spent the night on mattresses in barns and farm buildings. They claimed that they were kept awake all night in the big house by mysterious footsteps and banging doors. Amused at first by what he regarded as native superstition, the colonel went along with this arrangement for a while. But it was inconvenient for him, living alone in a huge house, to have no one during the hours of darkness.

In annoyance one day, he dismissed all the servants and hired new ones from distant places who would not have heard silly local gossip about his house. After a few weeks, the new servants began leaving or moving to barns at nighttime. They couldn't sleep in the house, they complained, because of the rattling, banging, and footsteps. One woman claimed to have seen a young girl dressed in white. The apparition vanished almost as soon as it appeared. The colonel tried to reason with them. He said he heard nothing and always slept soundly. Why couldn't they? Anyway, what harm could a young girl dressed in white do to them? He again found himself alone in the mansion at night.

The colonel had a friend who was interested in such things. He invited this man to stay as a guest and give his opinion. One night the guest woke the colonel from a deep sleep. Together, they listened to doors slamming, footsteps, and loud noises that seemed to be coming from the upper rooms. By candlelight, the two men investigated but saw nothing. Next morning, his guest recalled an urgent matter needing his immediate attention, regrettably cutting short his visit. The colonel said he understood and bade his friend goodbye.

That night he was alone in the house again. But this time, with a difference. Now he himself had heard footsteps and doors slamming. He left the lamp burning on a table beside his bed. The lamp had been filled with oil so that it would burn all night. Was this cowardice on his part? No, he decided, it was simply a soldier's prudence. It would be cowardice for him to give in to the impulse he was feeling so strongly—to run out of the house in his nightshirt and sleep in a barn with the servants! He would spend the night where he was. He was damned if he was going to be chased out of his home by a little girl dressed in white. . . .

The master bedroom was large and the oil lamp clearly illuminated only the area around the bed. The colonel lay sleepless and peered from time to time into the dark corners of the room. There was not a sound to be heard, but for his own breathing. Suddenly, at the foot of the bed, he saw the girl in white. She was hardly more than a child.

And she had a wound in her chest that was bleeding. She looked at him as if she were asking for help. Then, in front of his eyes, she faded into nothingness.

The old soldier jumped out of bed. He could handle this. Here was an injured child seeking his help. He grasped the lamp and searched the entire room. Finding nothing, he opened the bedroom door. He heard footsteps walking down the corridor floorboards. Gritting his teeth, he followed them. Holding the lamp to light his way, the colonel followed the footsteps up a flight of stairs to the attic. When he was halfway up the stairs, he saw the door to the attic open and loudly slam. He was tempted to run. But he controlled his fear and forced himself to climb the remaining stairs and open the attic door. He stepped inside and held the lamp aloft. There was nothing to see but cobwebbed piles of junk left by previous owners of the house. The colonel returned to his bedroom. Although he did not sleep that night, he heard no more footsteps or banging doors.

At first light, he returned to the attic and sorted through the junk. Eventually he found a small wood box that contained a metal box and a sheet of paper. The faded writing on the paper said that inside the metal box was the preserved heart of a daughter of the family that had previously owned the house. The colonel remembered the bleeding wound in the apparition's chest. He didn't like the sound of this.

Searching through a sheaf of old papers he had taken from the attic, he found a number of references to a young daughter who had fallen ill and been sent to a warm climate to recover. She died in Rome. As she lay dying, the girl spoke continually of home and begged that after her death, her heart would be buried at Glencairn. He found no explanation why her heart, after being brought home, had been left in the attic. The colonel was relieved, however, that nothing worse than carelessness was involved.

He buried the metal box wrapped in a yellow silk scarf in his favorite part of the garden. Since then the long nights at Glencairn have been peaceful. If the young girl has returned, no one has seen her.

69. The mouse is mistress in her own home.
70. The doorstep of a great house is slippery.
71. Wide is the door of a little cottage.
72. A hut is a palace to a poor man.
73. Have your own fire—or you'll need a lot of sunshine and no rain.

We will eat, so long as there is meat on the shin of a sparrow

Nearer, nearer wears the day that will see fell
Hunger, with stalking Plague in its train, over
this devoted land. From almost every county
in Ireland come reports of more and more
urgent alarm and terror, as the earthed-up
potatoes are uncovered, and found masses of
loathsome rottenness. . . . Galway, we learn,
is getting an additional military force; their
port lies wide open for the food to go out;
and if no provisions are coming in, there is at
least a war steamer in their harbour. Then as
for Westmeath, a man was to be hanged
there yesterday; if there is to be no adequate
means of supplying them with food, they
shall, at worst, have plenty of justice.

—*John Mitchel in the* Nation,
February 17, 1846

In a few years more, a Celtic Irishman will be as rare in Connemara as is the Red Indian on the shores of Manhattan.

> —*The London* Times, *cited in the Dublin* Freeman's Journal, *March 3, 1846*

Priests and patriots howl over the Exodus but the departure of thousands of papist Celts must be a blessing to the country they quit.

> —*Lord Clarendon, quoted in the* Nation, *March 14, 1846*

"Give us food or we perish" [is the cry] heard in every corner of the island—it breaks in like some awful spectre on the festive revelry of the licentious rich—it startles and appals the merchant at his desk, the landlord in his office, the scholar in his study, the lawyer in his stall, the minister in his council-room and the priest at the altar. It is a strange popular cry to be heard within the limits of the powerful and wealthy British empire. . . . Nothing but a state of being, in which the crimes of civilisation and barbarity had united to banish the virtues of both, could reduce a whole nation to a huge, untended poorhouse, from which only one prayer ascends—"Give us food or we perish."

—Belfast Vindicator, *October 5, 1846*

Owing to the extraordinary wetness of the season, turf cannot be procured—coals are out of the question, and the poor have thus the double pressure of hunger and cold to bear up against; while the rich wrap themselves up in their own importance and shun their dependants as a plague. The continual cry among the small farmers is, "What in the world are we to do!" The rent is being called for, in some instances, with merciless perseverance. Add the prospect of being turned out of their holdings, to that of depriving themselves of the means of sustenance, and you will be able to form an opinion of the feelings of the poor farmers of the district.

—Belfast Vindicator, *October 26, 1846*

Disease and death in every quarter—the once hardy population worn away to emaciated skeletons—fever, dropsy, diarrhoea and famine rioting in every filthy hovel and sweeping away whole families—the popula-

tion perceptibly lessened—death diminishing
the destitution . . . dead bodies of children
flung into holes hastily scratched in the earth
without shroud or coffin.

—Cork Examiner, *December 21, 1846*

Not a spark of fire on the hearths of nine out
of every ten of the wretched houses. And
where you do see a spark of fire, you will
behold the squalid and misery-stricken creatures crouching round it, like spectres, with
not a human lineament traceable upon their
countenances. As to food, good or bad, they
have none.

—Chronicle and Munster Advertiser,
March 22, 1847

In every seaport in Ireland are now thronging
thousands of farmers, with their families,
who have chosen to leave their lands untilled
and unsown, to sell horses and stock and
turn all into money to go to America, carry-
ing off both the money and the industry that
created it, and leaving a more hopeless mass
of misery and despair behind them. The
ground remains uncultivated because of
mutual distrust between landlord and tenant.

The landlord is afraid that, if he provides
seed, the tenant will consume the crop and
not pay his rent. The tenant is in dread that,
if he sows grain, the landlord will pounce on
the crop as soon as it is cut. . . . And the
doomed wretches, who can neither leave
their country nor live in it—when grubbed
up weeds will no longer sustain them, when
the agonies of hunger are over, and all the
bitterness of death is long past and gone,
patiently make themselves at home with
death—take their last look at the sun and the
blasted earth, and then wall themselves up in
their cabins, that they may die with their
children and not be seen by passers-by.

—*John Mitchel in the* Nation, *April 12, 1847*

Nothing is to be heard but lamentations, sighs
and moans, nothing scarcely to be seen but
crowds of emaciated, naked and starved creatures, flocking to every door, craving for
something to prolong life, even for a few
hours—but, alas, in vain. The people, however well disposed and ready to respond to
the calls of charity, are not able to give them
any, even the smallest relief, for such as were
hitherto in comparatively comfortable

circumstances, their private resources being
exhausted from purchasing food during the
year at an exorbitant price, are now reduced
to a level with almost the most destitute, thus
rendering almost universal that deluge of
ineffable woe which has visited this district.

—Fr. Malachy Duggan, parish priest of
Moyarta and Kilballyowen, County Clare,
in the Limerick Reporter, *May 17, 1847*

74. **You can't chew bread and whistle.**
75. **Never scald your lips with another man's porridge.**
76. **Soft words butter no parsnips.**
77. **I think little of buttermilk when I'm full of it.**
78. **Hunger is a good sauce.**
79. **One bit of rabbit is worth two bits of cat.**
80. **That's the stone in place of the egg.**

I MIGHT AS WELL WHISTLE JIGS TO A MILESTONE AS TELL MY TROUBLES TO YOU

American author James Charles Roy owns a ruined castle near Athenry, in the Galway countryside. One summer evening, as he and an old man approached the thatched cottage in which the old man lived, his mangy sheepdog ran out and bit Roy on the leg.

"God damn that worthless beast!" the old man shouted. "I'll give him the boot for ye."

When he saw that the dog's teeth had broken Roy's skin, he brought him inside the cottage to treat the wound. By candlelight, he poured whiskey from a bottle over the bite marks. Then, by way of apology, he offered Roy a swig from the bottle.

The following year Roy visited his friend again, this time successfully fending off the dog.

"He killed eight sheep last winter," the old man said, "and that cost me dear. I hadn't the heart to put him down, so I paid the neighbors, though it's you I blame. He decided when he got a taste of you in the summertime that he needed more mutton!"

81. Tell me your friends and I'll tell who you are.
82. If you walk with lame people, you will soon limp yourself.
83. There was never a scabby sheep in a flock that didn't want a companion.
84. If I like the sow, I like her litter.
85. A friend's coldness is better than an enemy's warmth.
86. The only people who are pleasant all the time are those with God in heaven.
87. Don't show your skin to someone who won't cover it.

88. Better to be alone than to be with those you don't like.
89. You don't really know people until you have shared a home with them.
90. A good friend's eyes are a reliable mirror.
91. Better to sit beside someone than in their place.

A closed hand is
a shut fist

Soon after 1170, the Norman knight Sir
Almeric de Tristram seized Howth, on
the north side of Dublin bay, from the
Viking settlers there. He took the family name of
St. Lawrence, because his success occurred on that
saint's feast day. Until recent years, the St. Lawrence
family continued to live in a castle there.

Grace O'Malley, the famed pirate queen of
Ireland's western coast, docked her ship at Howth
on her way home from visiting Queen Elizabeth
in London. Noting her lack of fondness for female
rivals, some people today doubt that Elizabeth
would have invited Grace, unless she wished to
intimidate her. Noting the treachery of the times,
others doubt that Grace would have come if she
were invited, unless she needed royal permission
to plunder someone's property. Perhaps they
underestimate the curiosity, love of life, and
courage of these two great ladies.

Arriving at Howth castle, Grace found the gate-house barred and was told to come back after the St. Lawrences had finished eating dinner. Insulted by this lack of hospitality, the pirate queen headed back to her ship. On the way, she saw a nurse-maid with a baby and was told that the infant was the St. Lawrence male heir. She took the child captive and brought him to her castle in County Mayo. To get him back, the St. Lawrences had to swear that their castle gates would never be shut at mealtimes and that a place would always be set at table for the chief of the O'Malleys. Over the succeeding centuries, the family kept these promises.

92. **The man who can't manage a loan is a great help otherwise.**
93. **The man who won't put you up for the night is good at giving directions.**
94. **Don't take the thatch off your own house to buy slates for another man's roof.**
95. **A big belly is never generous.**

96. They say a generous man has never gone to hell.
97. A gift giver who can't take his eyes off the gift he gave.
98. God's help is nearer than the door.
99. What can you expect from a pig but a grunt.
100. When you're up, expect loans—when you're down, expect stones.
101. When the hand ceases to scatter, the mouth ceases to praise.
102. A greedy person is always in need.
103. Necessity knows no hour.
104. Being poor spoils the pleasure of borrowing.

Blarney

The Blarney Stone is in the high battlements of the oldest part of Blarney castle, built in the mid-1400s. A short distance to the northwest of Cork city, the castle was erected as a MacCarthy stronghold. Queen Elizabeth was seizing the properties of Irish Catholic noblemen and giving them to Protestant favorites. She awarded the castle to Sir George Carew, whom she had appointed Lord President of Munster. Cormac MacDermot MacCarthy, the castle's owner, asked Sir George for a little time before moving out. Sir George consented. And Cormac stayed put. Next time Sir George asked him to leave, some minor inconvenience prevented Cormac from doing so. When Sir George got around once more to asking him to leave, Cormac replied it would be only a short while before he was gone. Then Sir George tried to be firm, but Cormac had a gift for sweet talk

and was very persuasive. Another complication
was the large number of grumpy MacDermots and
cantankerous MacCarthys staying as house guests
with Cormac. To Sir George, they looked just like
the sort of people who would create a fuss on
being asked to leave.

Sir George appealed to the queen. She sent a representative. This representative engaged in consultations with Cormac. He returned to London pleased
with the outcome of his consultations. Sir George
pointed out that Cormac was still in Blarney castle.
The queen sent higher level ministers. They held
fruitful negotiations with Cormac and they too
returned to London, satisfied with their endeavors.
While Sir George hated to make a pest of himself,
he felt he had to bring it to royal notice that Cormac
was still in the castle that the queen had awarded to
her loyal servant. This went on and on, until the
queen became exasperated.

"Blarney! Blarney!" she exclaimed petulantly. "I
will hear no more of this Blarney!"

And that was that. Cormac stayed on.

No one knows how the belief developed that
visitors can absorb some of Cormac's gift of the

gab by kissing a particular stone. To do so, they
have to be held by the legs at the castle top as
they lean out backward over a sheer drop to kiss
the stone. The belief goes back a long time. Father
Prout, the bogus priest who had more than a
touch of the Blarney himself and who was famous
for his song "The Bells of Shandon," published the
following song in 1860.

There is a stone there
That whoever kisses
Oh! he never misses
To grow eloquent.
'Tis he may clamber
To a lady's chamber
or become a member
Of parliament.
A clever spouter
He'll sure turn out, or
An out and outer
To be let alone.
Don't hope to hinder him
Sure he's a pilgrim
From the Blarney Stone.

105. A well is not valued till it runs dry.
106. However long a pitcher goes to the water, it is broken at last.
107. A lamb when carried far becomes as burdensome as a sheep.

A mouth of ivy and a heart of holly

Although they are traditional Christmas decorations and thus signs of celebration, ivy is poisonous and holly prickly.

The dictionary compiler Samuel Johnson said, "The Irish are a fair people; they never speak well of one another."

Men in ancient Ireland, unlike Irishmen today, were vain and quick to take offence. A king had to deal with the great power that wandering poets and scholars possessed to make fun of him before local rivals. Usually a king was willing to go to almost any length to avoid becoming the butt of a satire. Lavish welcomes, banquets, and gifts left kind memories in even the sharpest-tongued poet or scholar.

Some people say that a mixture of hospitality and satirical comments or gossip is a notable survivor of ancient times in Irish behavior today. A few years ago, an American friend and I sat at a table in a Dublin pub with seven or eight old friends of mine. Afterward my American friend said that, while she was impressed at my friends' generosity in buying rounds of drinks, she couldn't help noticing that each time someone left the table, someone else made a witty remark at that person's expense. She said she herself had badly wanted to go to the bathroom, but had been afraid to leave the table because of what someone might say about her while she was gone. While I don't think this would have prevented a Celtic warrior from relieving himself, he might have understood her situation.

108. A woman told me a woman told her she saw a woman who saw a woman make ale of potatoes.

109. Someone who brings you one bit of gossip will leave with two bits about yourself.

110. A whisper in a gossip's ear is louder than a shout.
111. A story that three people hear is no secret.
112. A kind word never broke anyone's mouth.
113. Don't let your tongue cut your throat.
114. A man's mouth can break his nose.
115. It's bad manners to talk about ropes in the house of a man who was hanged.
116. Walls have ears.
117. Trampling on dung only spreads it the more.
118. A silent mouth is sweet to hear.

The one who stays out of it sees the most of the fight

When a great Celtic warrior killed an opponent of equal stature in single combat, he often removed the man's brain tissue and mixed it with lime so that it formed a hard ball. If you had an argument with one of these warriors, he might have held a calcified brain in his hands to help his thinking process. When he put down the brain to free his sword hand would have been a good time to change the subject.

A Connacht warrior wandering Ulster stole the calcified brain of a hero who had been prophesied to bring great harm to Ulster. The hero had been killed without this prophecy being fulfilled. The Connacht warrior kept the stolen brain handy, in expectation that the prophecy might yet be fulfilled.

On a cattle raid in Ulster a while later, the same
Connacht warrior was chased and cornered by
Ulster warriors. He decided to keep the stolen
cattle and fight his way out of Ulster. As the
confrontation built, warriors flocked to each side,
bringing their entourages of beautiful women,
harpists, and bards. The Ulster king joined the
Ulstermen to see some action.

The Ulster king was widely known to be the
handsomest man in all Ireland. The beautiful
Connacht women had heard about him and were
curious to see him for themselves. They sent word
to him. Like any man would, the Ulster king felt
obliged to satisfy the women's curiosity. But the
Connacht warrior had heard about their meeting.
From a distance, he watched the handsome Ulster
king charm the beautiful Connacht women. As he
watched, he loaded the slain hero's calcified brain
into a slingshot, whirled the slingshot, and sent
the brain stone on a journey through the air. It
struck the Ulster king on top of the head.

The Ulster king's doctors and sorcerers saved his
life, but the brain stone had to remain embedded
in his skull. His chief doctor sewed up the wound

around it with thread the same gold color as the king's hair. But the king could not live anymore as he always had. He was now disfigured. The doctors forbade him to enter a warrior's frenzy, ride a horse, make love to a woman, eat gluttonously, or run.

The Ulster king lived in the absence of these things for seven years. Then one day a great rage overcame him. He grasped his sword and, in a warrior's frenzy, cut and slashed at the trees until the forest was bare around him. This exertion knocked the brain stone out of his skull and the Ulster king fell dead.

119. An Irishman is never at peace except when he's fighting.
120. Put an Irishman on a spit and you'll find two more to turn him.
121. End a party rather than begin a fight.
122. Wine is better than blood.
123. Don't show your teeth to someone you can't bite.

124. Someone can die between two words.
125. A word goes to the wind, but a blow goes to the bone.
126. A fight between hornless sheep.
127. To someone ready for war, peace is assured.
128. Peace is better even than winning an easy war.

To every cow her calf, and to every book its copy

About thirteen hundred years ago in an Ulster monastery, a monk arrived from Rome with a rare book. In those days, even books with little artistic merit were extremely valuable. Each book was copied by hand from another onto fine-grained calfskin (vellum), and this required many hours of craftsmanship.

The monks gathered around to examine this new treasure. Among them was a visiting monk named Columcille, a brilliant nobleman with powerful connections who had chosen to live a humble life. Columcille had his own monastery, at a site on which the present city of Derry is built. He decided his monastery needed this new book, but the abbot denied his request to copy it.

Very late one night, a curious monk noticed
light from beneath the door of Columcille's cell.
He peered through the keyhole and saw
Columcille copying the new book. The monk realized that Columcille had been bringing the new
book to his cell every night in order to surreptitiously copy it for his own use, despite the abbot's
order forbidding it. This passed through his mind
an instant before Columcille's pet heron thrust its
daggerlike bill through the keyhole and pecked
out his eye. Screaming with pain, the monk
roused the monastery.

Columcille had to hand over the new book but
claimed ownership of the nearly complete copy he
had made. The abbot insisted that the unautho-
rized copy belonged to him. The case was brought
before the king, who looked at the calfskin pages
and made the world's first copyright decision: To
every cow her calf, and to every book its copy.

The king's decision was taken by Columcille as a
personal insult. The same king added to this insult
when he broke the sanctuary of Columcille's
monastery by capturing and executing a man that
the monk had given shelter to. The man was

wanted for killing at the time of a royal council, for the duration of which the king had declared it illegal to kill enemies. This was too much for Columcille. He raised an army and met the king's forces in a bloody battle. Columcille was the victor.

Afterward he walked the battlefield and counted three thousand men lying dead. Now he saw them as the fruit of his own greed, pride and anger. Columcille went to a solitary holy man for spiritual guidance. The holy man said he must leave Ireland forever and make as many converts to Christianity as he had caused deaths on the battlefield. Columcille left his beloved Derry and settled on Iona, an island off Scotland, just out of sight of Ireland on even the clearest day.

129. **Innocent or guilty, he'll hang, said the judge.**
130. **It's no joke suing the devil when the court is in hell.**
131. **You can't sue for the blow not struck.**

The shameless thrive where the shame-faced die

When foot-and-mouth disease occurred on the Cooley peninsula in County Louth early in 2001, thousands of sheep had to be killed to stop the spread of the infectious animal ailment. The farmers who owned the sheep were promised government compensation. But the government later had problems with fully half of the claims. According to the Department of Agriculture, thirty percent of claimants exaggerated the number of sheep they had owned, another fifteen percent wildly exaggerated that number, and five percent had never owned any sheep at all.

On June 19, 2001, as reported in the *Irish Times*, about a hundred farmers from the Cooley peninsula picketed government buildings to demand additional compensation. They said they also wanted rogue farmers to be prosecuted. Their spokesman said that the Department of Agriculture accusations were totally unfounded and had cast a slur on the many decent farmers in the area who were being held up to ridicule.

"We hold no torch for those few people who were involved in fraud and we disassociate ourselves from them," he said. "But to lump the rest of the farmers on the Cooley peninsula into the same barrow is just too much."

132. **Bribe the rogue and you need have no fear of the honest man.**
133. **When rogues quarrel, honest people do well.**
134. **A thief sees the world as full of thieves.**
135. **The greatest thief makes the best hangman.**

It doesn't take much wind to move giddy people

A woman teacher at an Elderhostel in Indiana told Maureen Dezell, a staff writer for the *Boston Globe*, that she cringed at the sight of a man in a white Aran sweater, green checked pants and a green tam-o'-shanter with an orange bauble on top. It wasn't even St. Patrick's Day! The teacher resigned herself when she was stuck with this man and his wife on a class trip. He made her dislike him even more when he expressed his political opinions. Although he didn't seem to know much about what was happening and had no grasp of the complexities, he was fervent in his support of violence as a solution to differences in Northern Ireland. She decided he was a perfect specimen of the kind of Irish American that she couldn't stand.

He told the teacher about his and his wife's trip to Ireland. They traveled in style, with a set of new matching bags and a big rental car. They were a little surprised that Irish people didn't seem to warm to them immediately. Noticing that hitchhikers to whom they gave rides spoke to them more willingly than other people, they decided from this that they should become hitch-hikers too. They turned in the big car and set out on the road.

The teacher tried to visualize them standing on the side of a narrow country road in their "native costume" of plaids and tam-o'-shanters, with their coordinated luggage stacked beside them. She said it never seemed to have occurred to them that no one else in Ireland looked like they did. They had a great time and met dozens of people. Listening to their adventures, the teacher felt her dislike turn into a strong liking.

This pair must have been just what the locals needed on a slow day in County Offaly.

136. Giving advice to a fool is like giving cherries to pigs.
137. Even a fool has luck.
138. Big head, little sense.
139. Everyone needs to break some glass, the fool said.
140. When a fool chooses, expect a foolish choice.
141. His feeding has been better than his thinking.

A GENTLEMAN IS A MAN WHO OWNS BAGPIPES BUT NEVER PLAYS THEM

The resting place of King Arthur may instead be the birthplace of Saint Patrick.

Legend has it that Arthur and Guinevere are buried in the cathedral, now ruins, of the Somerset town of Glastonbury. This legend is based on the finding of a man and woman buried together where the cathedral once stood, but there's little historical probability that they were King Arthur and Queen Guinevere. It's reasonably possible, however, that Patrick's father, a romanized Celt, was a priest at this cathedral and his family would have lived within its enclosure. Having been seized there as a child by Irish raiders and sold into slavery in Ulster, Patrick may have returned to Glastonbury, where he became a priest himself.

Knowing Ireland's customs, Patrick used the immunity from harm granted to traveling poets and scholars to carry word of Christianity through the many small Gaelic kingdoms. Patrick must have had a forceful personality and great powers of persuasion to challenge the values of Celtic warriors. One story illustrates what some of his future parishioners were like. One day Patrick was physically exhausted by the time a local king was ready to be baptized as a Christian. He leaned wearily on his bishop's staff as he poured water over the royal head. It was only when he had finished that Patrick noticed the pointed end of his staff had penetrated the king's deerskin shoe and pinned his foot to the ground. Appalled, Patrick gently withdrew the staff from the man's foot.

Patrick looked in the king's impassive face. "Why didn't you say something?" he asked.

"Weren't you testing me to see if my face would show pain?" the king asked. "I thought it was part of becoming a Christian."

142. An empty bag won't stand.
143. You can't take more out of a bag than all its contents.
144. As lazy as a piper's little finger.
145. Like a bagpipe, he won't make noise till his belly is full.

A witch to the senses . . .

"A witch to the senses, a demon to the soul, a thief to the purse, the wife's woe, the husband's misery, the parent's disgrace, the children's sorrow and the beggar's companion"

The above words were used in 1823 by Father Henry Young, an early temperance worker in Dublin. The temperance movement got under way seriously about six years later. But not everything went smoothly. Clergymen complained to the authorities that teetotallers and their marching bands outside churches on Sunday made such a racket that they disturbed divine worship. Policemen interrupting one band in mid-tune were attacked by the band members. Other disturbances and assaults occurred. With the churches and streets in an uproar, you can imagine that this must have provided some thirsty Dubliners with a good excuse to slip into a pub for a little peace and quiet.

In 1876, a Select Committee of the House of Lords on Intemperance was appointed to investigate Dublin public houses. Testimony was heard from all sides. One witness, a judge, sounded a bit irate—and perhaps a little over the top:

> Dublin is saturated with drink, it is flooded with drink, it is the staple manufacture. Every kind of drink which the people care to consume is manufactured in unlimited quantities in Dublin. Every third or fourth house deals in drink.

Another witness told the committee:

> Public houses are chiefly established, I think, for the use of those who have no private houses, and two-thirds of the population of Dublin have literally no dwellings, no private houses. They have simply a place to sleep in. . . . What are they to do? They cannot go and sit on the flags in the open street. . . .

One sporting gentleman defended the Dublin poor, though perhaps not in terms that they would have appreciated:

> Thousands upon thousands of the multitudes in this city live and die in places whence a humane sportsman would be ashamed to whistle forth his spaniels. Surely it is vain that I, or such as I, should bid them, steeped in squalor and besieged by disease, joyless, hopeless, Godless, not to seek the light and warmth of the gin-palace, and the oblivion, however temporary and baneful, they can purchase therein.

The select committee was not amused.

Only two kinds of women used to be welcome in Dublin pubs. "Grannies could go in because they were beyond sin," a woman told Kevin C. Kearns, author of *Dublin Pub Life and Lore: An Oral History*. The other kind were women street market dealers, who couldn't be kept out because they could outdrink, outcurse, and outbrawl most men. Kearns' informant told him that the pubs around the Liberties in Dublin used to be so dirty and dismal, most women didn't *want* to go in them.

> Your first impression was that pubs were hor-
> rible and there was sawdust all over the place
> and the men just spit everywhere and they'd
> urinate everywhere. There was no hygiene at
> all. And the smell of smoke and tobacco!
> They chewed tobacco, so when they weren't
> drinking they were spitting. And TB was
> rampant then. I mean it was disgusting. I
> used to be horrified with it.

When American bars and clubs that had previously refused admission to women finally admitted them, women found that provision of a ladies' room was often not a priority of the management. Women street market dealers handled a similar situation in Dublin pubs a few generations ago. "They'd have to go out in the street," a one-time pub owner told Kearns. "Yes, in the open street. Over the street grating in front of the pub. They wore skirts down to their ankles and they didn't wear any underwear."

In case it needs to be said, present-day male and female visitors to Dublin will find the circumstances described here much changed.

146. It was the first drop that destroyed me,
so there's no harm at all in the last.
147. Whiskey makes a rabbit spit at a dog.
148. The devil couldn't do it unless he was
drunk.
149. A drink is shorter than a story.
150. Seldom are hunger and thirst found
together.

The river is no wider from this side than the other

At sixteen, in 1999, Sarah Flannery from Cork won Ireland's Young Scientist of the Year Award. By that age, she had also developed an international reputation as a computer hacker—someone with the ability, among other things, to make uninvited visits to institutional computer networks. Her mathematical abilities and familiarity with privacy problems on the Internet got her a job with Baltimore Technologies, a leading electronic data security firm. Sarah left Cork to work in the Dublin company. While there, she continued to unravel the mathematical intricacies of a process to speed up encryption of data over the Internet. On her completion of the process, named the Cayley-Purser algorithm, she refused

to copyright it, believing that it should be free to
all. The process is now in worldwide use. Sarah is
studying at Cambridge University and has published a book.

151. You can't draw blood out of a turnip.
152. Never a door shut but another opened.
153. In for a penny, in for a pound.
154. You might as well be hung for a sheep as
a lamb.
155. It's hard to choose between two blind
goats.
156. Time and patience bring the snail to
Jerusalem.
157. Though you've broken the bone, you've
not sucked the marrow.
158. The tools are half the trade.
159. To make a beginning is one-third of the
work.
160. Strike while the iron is hot.
161. A good run is better than a long stand.
162. Seek one thing and you will find another.

163. Two days in spring are worth ten days in harvest.
164. The one who eats the meat drinks the broth.
165. It is a long road that has no turn in it.
166. He who doesn't work for himself has to work for others.
167. A little fire that warms is better than a big fire that burns.
168. What kills one man gives life to another.

Lying in Lavender like Paddy's pig

doe Castle, on a rocky headland on Sheephaven Bay in County Donegal, was built by the MacSweenys on land they received as payment as mercenaries for the O'Donnells. In 1544 a MacSweeny killed his brother for the castle. He in turn was killed not long afterward, as was the son who succeeded him. These ownership issues continued to be resolved within the family, until Sir Miles MacSweeny sided with the English.

The powerful Red Hugh O'Donnell evicted Sir Miles from the castle, after which Sir Miles saw the error of his ways and repented. Red Hugh permitted him to return to Doe Castle, but insisted that he share it with his cousin Owen MacSweeny. Later, while Sir Miles was away, Owen sided with the English. With English help, he successfully defended the castle against a joint siege by Red Hugh and Sir Miles. Afterward, the Crown for some reason awarded the castle to Red Hugh's brother, Rory O'Donnell. In a fury, Owen switched sides back to the Irish, but was captured by the English and executed in 1605.

While Rory O'Donnell's back was turned, Niall MacSweeny—Owen's brother—occupied the castle. Rory evicted him. Then Rory sailed into exile in 1607, never to return. This permitted Sir Miles MacSweeny to retake Doe Castle with Irish allies.

Are you following this?

The English captured the castle in 1611, but lost it thirty years later to Captain Donnell MacSweeny, a son of Niall. The English took the castle again nine years later. Colonel Miles MacSweeny—a grandson of Sir Miles—offered to change sides if the English would give him the castle. Having perhaps become a little suspicious by now, they refused. They lost the castle to Donogh Oge MacSweeny—a grandson of Colonel Miles—in 1689.

Doe Castle became uninhabited during the 1700s. In the early 1800s the Harte family repaired it and gave shelter to an impoverished itinerant tinsmith named Eamon MacSwyne, a grandson or great-grandson of Donogh Oge.

During the late 1800s, the castle again became uninhabited. A Gaelic festival held there in 1905 was attended by thousands, who were led to the castle by a piper playing "McSwyne's March." The piper's skills had won him fame at the Chicago World Fair in 1896. His name was Turlogh MacSweeny.

169. **Good luck is better than early rising.**

170. **Better to be lucky than wise.**

171. **Better to be idle than work for nothing.**

172. **Make sure to ask a lazy person to bring you bad news.**

173. **The long stitch of the lazy tailor.**

174. **Laziness is a heavy burden.**

175. **It's hard to tell which is better—speed or delay.**

176. **What you don't have to do is more fun to do.**

177. If there was work in the bed, he'd sleep on the floor.
178. May the wind of prosperity be always at your back.

Misfortune

A seventy-one-year-old woman's wrist was broken when she was battered to the ground by a swan in Dublin's Phoenix Park. She sued the state for personal injuries.

As reported in the *Irish Times* on Friday, May 25, 2001, she told the judge that after she had fed the swan, she turned away and heard a fluttering of wings behind her. "He was coming for me," she said. "He knocked me to the ground. He continued to aggressively beat my legs with his wings and tried to peck me on the head."

Someone nearby startled the swan by blowing a car horn, and this gave the woman a chance to get inside her own car. The swan then attacked her car, pecking at it and beating it with his wings.

A retired park foreman testified that he often saw the bird being fed by the public. "I never knew him to be a rogue or vicious swan," he said.

An expert on swans testified that they are passive, attacking only when their eggs or young are threatened.

The court was told that the cock swan may have been looking for a mate. The judge, while accepting that swans are not given to menacing behavior, decided that this individual had been having a very bad day and launched an attack on the woman. "It may well be that she had the bag of food," the judge said, "and the swan, like Oliver Twist, came back looking for more and beat her to the ground."

In denying the woman's injuries action, the judge said that the park commissioners had not acquired a wild jungle beast and permitted it to roam free. The swan had flown into the park of its own accord. Because the park commissioners had allowed the public to enjoy the bird's presence did not mean that they had assumed ownership and responsibility for its actions.

The swan was captured and released on an estuary some distance from the city.

179. In slender currents comes good luck, but in roaring torrents comes misfortune.
180. Misfortune matches fortune, inch for inch.
181. Out of the pot, into the fire.
182. You have come the day after the fair.
183. There's worse than this in the North.
184. Many a defect is noticed in a poor person.
185. Wait till I fall before you lift me.
186. There's often great darkness with little rain.
187. It's their own wounds people feel soonest.
188. Poverty destroys punctuality.
189. No woe to want.
190. A beggar is in no danger from a robber.
191. He whose fate it is to be hanged will never be drowned.

Falsehood goes further than truth

Shallardstown House was built in the early 1800s, not far from the scenic Vee pass in Tipperary's Galty mountains. The house was built by Cadogan and Angelica Parrott. They had two daughters, Angelica and Rosaleen. Their mother committed suicide, followed shortly by their father. The eldest daughter, Angelica, inherited everything. While the older girl was now rich and independent, the younger was beautiful. Angelica fell in love with a handsome but penniless local gentleman named Dagan Ferritter. Although Dagan badly wanted Shallardstown House, he wanted the beautiful younger sister, Rosaleen, even more. They married in 1837.

To get them out of her sight, Angelica gave the newly married pair a very modest allowance on condition that they disappear to France, Italy, or

Spain. When they were gone, the loneliness of the house and the empty mountain wilderness became too much for her. Angelica went to live in London. While there, she married Prince Nicholas Orloff, who was on the staff of the Russian embassy. They visited St. Petersburg and then went to live in Paris.

But Prince Nicholas soon died in Paris and Princess Angelica returned to Shallardstown House, draped in widow's black. She dismissed all the servants, except Creed, the butler. He became her only contact with the outside world. On the stroke of three every afternoon, with Creed as coachman, she went for a drive. Local men tipped their hats as the coach passed, getting no response from the reclusive princess seated inside. The coach always returned promptly on the stroke of four.

Rosaleen and Dagan wearied of traveling around Europe with little money. They returned to Shallardstown House, hoping for a reconciliation between the sisters. Angelica ordered them out of the house. Hoping to embarrass her into a show of generosity, they moved into a little cottage nearby and lived humbly. The princess ignored them.

As the years went by, Dagan became obsessed with becoming master of Shallardstown. He and the beautiful Rosaleen waited and waited, but nothing changed. They had nowhere to go and continued to subsist on the miserable allowance Angelica permitted them. Finally, after many years, Dagan couldn't take it anymore. He rode to the front door, pushed his way in past the butler and demanded to see Angelica so that he could talk with her.

"You may see the princess, sir," Creed said, "but you cannot talk with her."

"I will!" Dagan shouted.

"Impossible, sir," the butler said. "She's been dead for eleven years."

Creed produced Angelica's written instructions that he was to drive her body around every day exactly as he had done when she was alive.

Furious at the dead woman whose deceit delayed their inheritance, Rosaleen and Dagan moved immediately into the big house. They intended to make up for lost time by living in high style. Within a year, both were dead.

192. As great a liar as the clock of Strabane.
193. Truth is bitter, but a lie is savory at
     times.
194. The liar deceives the greedy man.

As old as Atty Hayes' goat

A twell (Atty) Hayes was a very old Corkman who owned a goat that was said to be even older than himself. The goat died of old age shortly after Atty's granddaughter's husband was elected lord mayor of Cork city in 1800. The new mayor announced that venison would be the main course at his inaugural banquet. Atty's goat was served as venison. None of the fawning office-seekers at the banquet complained about the food, and the mayor made sure that they finished everything on their plates.

195. As hairy as a puck goat's head.
196. A ring on her finger and rags on her back.
197. A small stain smears white stockings.

198. The wearer knows best where the shoe pinches.
199. If you have to wear rags, wear clean rags.
200. A coat so worn, sheep could eat the grass through it.
201. As long as a wet Sunday.
202. An inch is a great deal in a man's nose.
203. Handsome is as handsome does.
204. Beef to the heels like a Mullingar heifer.
205. More hair than tit, like a mountain heifer.

The herb that can't be got is the one that brings relief

A translation of the following Gaelic song was first published in Dublin in 1789 in Charlotte Brooke's *Reliques of Irish Poetry*. The translation here is modified from Kenneth Hurlstone Jackson's. The original anonymous Gaelic song may be three or four hundred years old, and possibly much older.

> She's the white flower of the blackberry, she's the sweet flower of the raspberry, she's the best herb I could ever find to improve my eyesight.
>
> She's my pulse, she's my secret, she's the scented flower of the apple, she's summer in the cold time between Christmas and Easter.

Love and herbs are closely allied in the Irish tradition. There are potions to make the person you
love fall in love with you—and potions also to
make your enemy develop spectacular symptoms.
Today "healers" try to palm you off with remedies
for minor ailments. You must persist to make
them give you the powerful stuff.

206. Though honey is sweet, don't lick it off
thorns.

207. A good laugh and a long sleep beat a
doctor's remedies.

208. If butter or whiskey can't cure it,
nothing can.

The stars make no noise

Patriot and revolutionary Robert Emmet, aged twenty-five, was convicted of high treason in a one-day trial at the Sessions House in Dublin on Monday, September 19, 1803. He made a brilliant speech from the dock before being sentenced to be hanged at dawn the next day. The chief judge, Lord Norbury, repeatedly interrupted him. In his final interruption, Norbury suggested that Emmet's father, were he still alive, would not agree with his son's political views. Emmet replied as follows.

> If the spirits of the illustrious dead participate in the concerns and cares of those who were dear to them in this transitory life, Oh, ever dear and venerated shade of my departed father, look down with scrutiny upon the conduct of your suffering son, and see if I have, even for a moment, deviated from those principles of morality and patriotism

which it was your care to instil into my
youthful mind, and for which I am now
about to offer up my life.

My lords, you seem impatient for the sacri-
fice. The blood for which you thirst is not
congealed by the artificial terrors which sur-
round your victim—it circulates warmly and
unruffled through the channels which God
created for noble purposes, but which you
are now bent to destroy, for purposes so
grievous that they cry to heaven. Be yet
patient! I have but a few words more to say.

I am going to my cold and silent grave. My
lamp of life is nearly extinguished. My race is
run. The grave opens to receive me, and I
sink into its bosom. I have but one request to
ask at my departure from this world. It is: the
charity of its silence.

Let no man write my epitaph. For as no
man who knows my motives dare now
vindicate them, let not prejudice or ignorance
asperse them. Let them and me rest in
obscurity and peace, and my name remain
uninscribed, until other times and other men
can do justice to my character. When my
country takes her place among the nations of
the earth, then, and not till then, let my
epitaph be written. I have done.

209. Many a day we shall rest in the clay.
210. Beginning with a cough and ending with a coffin.
211. There'll be many a dry eye at his funeral.
212. What would shame him would turn back a funeral.
213. Death stares the old in the face and lurks behind the back of the young.

BETTER TO DO A GOOD DEED AND BE BOASTFUL THAN DO NOTHING AND BE QUIET ABOUT IT

John Pentland Mahaffy, who became a fellow of Dublin University in 1864 and provost in 1915, domineered the scholars' dinner table by holding forth at length on every subject under the sun. His caustic wit made interruption unwise. Five of the scholars decided to do something about this intolerable situation. They agreed to choose a subject that Mahaffy couldn't possibly know anything about, read about it themselves and then discuss it in detail throughout dinner. They consulted a volume of the *Encyclopedia Britannica* at random. The pages fell open to a long article on Chinese music. As they read, they assigned discussion points among themselves for dinner that night.

The discussion went well. Scholars at the long table who were not part of the conspiracy soon guessed what was up and surreptitiously glanced at Mahaffy, waiting for him to quell this rebellion. But the great man concentrated on his food in silence, seemingly defeated by the voluble connoisseurs of oriental music.

At the end of dinner, Mahaffy scraped the legs of his chair on the floor as he stood and looked contemptuously down the table at the five scholars. He said, "Gentlemen, I *wrote* that encyclopedia article."

214. **It's bad to listen to no advice, but worse to listen to all advice.**
215. **Don't be too modest about yourself, because others may take you at face value.**
216. **Don't knock your shin against something that's not in your way.**

217. It's easier to scatter than to gather.
218. Praise the ripe field, not the green corn.
219. Better to be envied than pitied.
220. A blanket is the warmer for being
     doubled.

If it hasn't been eaten and hasn't been stolen, it will be found

One day the monks were holding a meeting at Clonmacnois, a large settlement on the river Shannon. They were amazed to see a ship in full sail above them, moving through the air. The men on the ship looked down and pointed at the monks on the ground. One threw an anchor over the side. Several monks held on to the anchor where it fell to stop it dragging over the ground. The ship came to a stop above them. Then one of the men in the ship dived over the side and swam down through the air as if he were swimming through water. He tried to pull the anchor from the monks' grasp, but they held on to it.

"Let it go!" the man shouted to them. "You're drowning me!"

They released the anchor.

The man held the anchor beneath one arm and used his other arm to swim upward through the air to the ship. The others helped him on board. The ship then sailed away.

Allowing for the images and technology of a thousand years ago, this account sounds quite like some modern spaceship visitations. The story made a strong impression back then, enough for it to be repeated in a thirteenth-century Norse account.

This incident does not involve typical Celtic exaggeration. The ship is simple and its crew behave without warrior bravado. The story doesn't seem to involve a monastic parable or hallucination of religious significance. But it might be a mistake to dismiss the story as a medieval fantasy. One incident long assumed to be medieval fantasy has been discovered to be factual. St. Brendan the Navigator's account of his voyage to North America in the sixth century describes an attack on his boat by "sea monsters." English writer Tim Severin repeated the sea journey in order to show that it could have been done in Brendan's time and that an Irish monk was the first Western discoverer of North America. As accurately as he could, Severin duplicated Brendan's equipment, including his cowskin coracle boat. Severin's voyage succeeded, but was nearly fatally terminated in mid-ocean by a pod of killer whales. These predators were attracted by chemical messengers from the boat's cowhide skin long soaking in water—the killer whales assumed, reasonably enough, that it was a large, helpless, floating animal. Their appearance and attack behavior closely matched those of the "sea monsters" in Brendan's account so many centuries ago.

I have no idea what might account for a boat floating over Clonmacnois, but I couldn't have explained Brendan's sea monsters either.

221. Nearest to chapel, latest to Mass.
222. There are many kinds of musical instru-
ments, said the man with the stick and
empty bottle.

223. He has both ends of the rope and permission to pull.
224. He doesn't hear what isn't pleasing to him.
225. The more important the messenger, the bigger the news.
226. He has more than lice in his head.
227. He knows how many beans make five.
228. He comes like bad weather, uninvited.

May God keep
you in his hand
and never close
his fist too tight
on you.

Background
Reading

J. D. Biersdorfer, "Among code warriors, women, too, can
fight," *New York Times*, June 7, 2001.

Angela Bourke, *The Burning of Bridget Cleary: A True Story*,
New York: Viking, 2000.

Brian de Breffny, *Castles of Ireland*, London: Thames &
Hudson, 1977.

Thomas Cahill, *How the Irish Saved Civilization: The Untold
Story of Ireland's Heroic Role from the Fall of Rome to the
Rise of Medieval Europe*, New York: Nan A.
Talese/Doubleday, 1995.

Maureen Dezell, *Irish America: Coming into Clover*, New
York: Doubleday, 2001.

N. Donnelly, *Short Histories of Dublin Parishes*, part XV:
Parish of Howth and Baldoyle, Blackrock, Co. Dublin:
Carraig, reprint.

John J. Dunne, *Haunted Ireland: Her Romantic and
Mysterious Ghosts*, Dublin: Appletree, 1977.

Laurence Flanagan, *Irish Proverbs*, Dublin: Gill &
Macmillan, 1995.

Sarah Flannery with David Flannery, *In Code: A
Mathematical Journey*, New York: Workman, 2001.

Sean Gaffney and Seamus Cashman (eds.), *Proverbs and
Sayings of Ireland*, Dublin: Wolfhound, 1974.

Sharon Gmelch, *Nan: The Life of an Irish Travelling Woman*,
    New York: Norton, 1986.

Marie Heaney, *Over Nine Waves: A Book of Irish Legends*,
    London: Faber & Faber, 1994.

Joan Hoff and Marian Yeates, *The Cooper's Wife Is Missing:
    The Trials of Bridget Cleary*, New York: Basic Books,
    2000.

Hans Holzer, *The Lively Ghosts of Ireland*, New York: Ace,
    1967.

Kenneth Hurlstone Jackson, *A Celtic Miscellany: Translations
    from the Celtic Literatures*, London: Routledge & Kegan
    Paul, 1951.

Kevin C. Kearns, *Dublin Pub Life and Lore: An Oral History*,
    Niwot, Colorado: Roberts Rinehart, 1997.

Sean MacConnell, "Cooley farmers seek extra payments,"
    Irish Times, June 20, 2001.

James Mackay, *Michael Collins: A Life*, Edinburgh:
    Mainstream, 1996.

Frank McNally, "The hero of Aintree laps it up like a true
    Christian," *Irish Times*, April 10, 2000.

Ray Managh, "Woman victim of swan's attack loses injury
    claim," *Irish Times*, May 25, 2001.

Kuno Meyer (transl.), *Selections from Ancient Irish Poetry*,
    London: Constable, 1911.

Brendan O Cathaoir, *Famine Diary*, Dublin: Irish Academic
    Press, 1999.

Brian O Cuiv (ed.), *A View of the Irish Language*, Dublin:
    Stationery Office, 1969.

Robert Emmet, Dublin: Kilmainham Jail Historical Museum,
    1978.

Tim Robinson, *Stones of Aran: Pilgrimage*, Dublin:
    Lilliput/Wolfhound, 1986.

James Charles Roy, *The Fields of Athenry: A Journey Through Irish History*, Boulder, Colorado: Westview/Perseus, 2001.

Tim Severin, *The Brendan Voyage*, New York: Modern Library Exploration Series, 2000.

Brian M. Walker, Art O'Broin, and Sean McMahon, *Faces of Ireland*, New York: Amaryllis, 1984.

Lyn Webster Wilde, *Celtic Women: In Legend, Myth and History*, London: Blandford/Cassell, 1997.